LAUGHING CAMERA

A *terra magica* BOOK

HANNS REICH

Laughing Camera

Text by Heinz Held

HILL and WANG · NEW YORK

It is a sense of humor that we enjoy most directly, for this good trait is its own reward. The cheerful man always has a good reason for being cheerful: namely, the very fact that he is cheerful. No other human trait can replace any other good so completely as a sense of humor, which itself is irreplaceable.

SCHOPENHAUER

My uncle was always quoting. Golden phrases rolled about in his mouth like cherry pits. "Hoping against hope," "apple of his eye," "money doesn't smell"–he knew Bartlett by heart. It was awful.

As I began writing this introduction, I thought of my kind-hearted but unbearable Uncle Otto. He would always say, "Life is grave, art is humorous." He was certainly no photographer, because for this breed of men, exactly the reverse is true: life is humorous–at times–and art, i.e., three-dimensional life on film, is grave. By which I mean to say, photographers can't tell jokes. They lack the cartoonist's gift for transforming grotesque ideas directly into real pictures. Photographers can't change the silhouettes of their subjects. They can't distort natural proportions at will to suit emotional or intellectual interpretations as caricaturists can to provoke laughter. For a photographer, an amusing idea must be posed, which means that he has to "construct and drape" or have it acted out. But this has less to do with photography than with the art of decorating, staging, acting. If cameras or laboratory equipment are employed, it turns into a matter of physics and chemistry. Even photographic distortions produced by special mirrors (such as the American photographer Wegee uses) are merely clever gags and not true humor. My dear departed uncle would merely quote Goethe: "Just another silly gimmick."

No. Photographers cannot produce humor, wit, or comedy. They have to track it down in real life. The cartoonist depends on inspiration, the photographer on chance. The ingenious cartoonist is one who has ideas, the ingenious photographer is one who sees something. After all, there is no shortage of humor. Comic elements often congeal into a funny optical figuration: a similarity between a man and an animal, the proximity of like objects, the meeting of unlike objects, an optical illusion, the contrast between big and little, round and angular, and so forth. But there must always be a modicum of reconciliation to prevent the polarities from turning into nasty irony.

Sometimes, by making a movement freeze into a grotesque form, the camera can project a joke into our visual field. Such momentary petrification of movement and the accompanying transformation of the natural into the artificial is, in my opinion, something specifically photographic. Therein lies the strength of the camera artist. No one else can emulate him. But it is a very difficult feat. The mechanical registration of an action does not necessarily result in a picture. Akin to the pictures of other visual media, a photographic shot becomes a picture only when the combination of tones, silhouettes, and proportions reaches a certain tension that is hard to describe, but essential for the snapshot to become a picture. In other words, in the moment of seeing, the photographer must simultaneously conceive and construct the picture.

Naturally, the ability to react lightning fast is not enough. A fine sense for the amusing aspects of life is indispensable.

Without this "sensitive nerve" the photographer will have a hard time finding comic motifs. I myself, for example, have to look and look and look, eaten up by envy of my merry colleagues. No matter what I do, even my amusing pictures look sad. I guess I'm just a melancholy guy. What can you do . . . ?

Translated by Joachim Neugroschel

Table of photographs

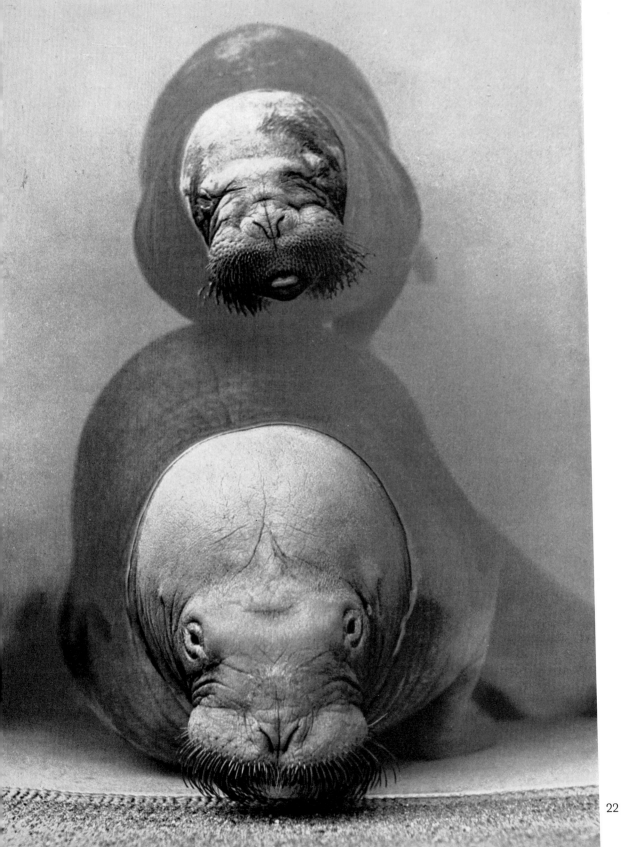

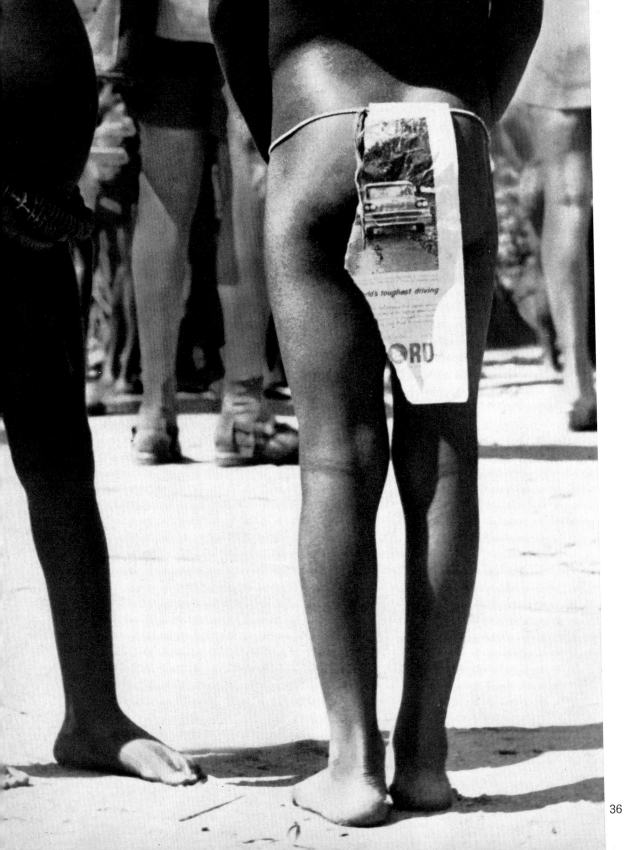

40

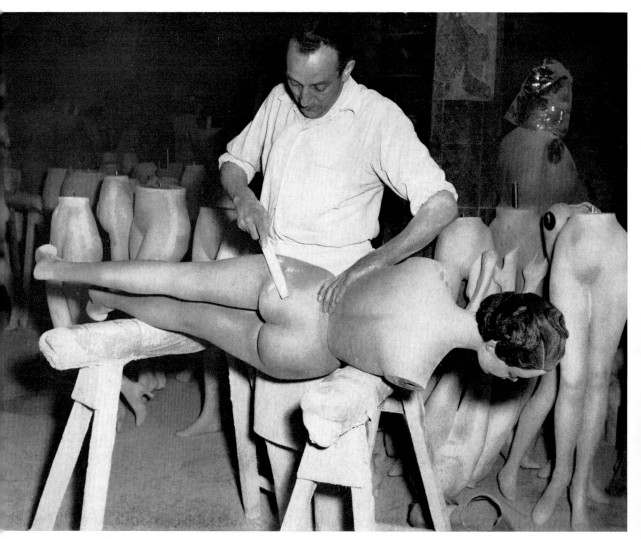

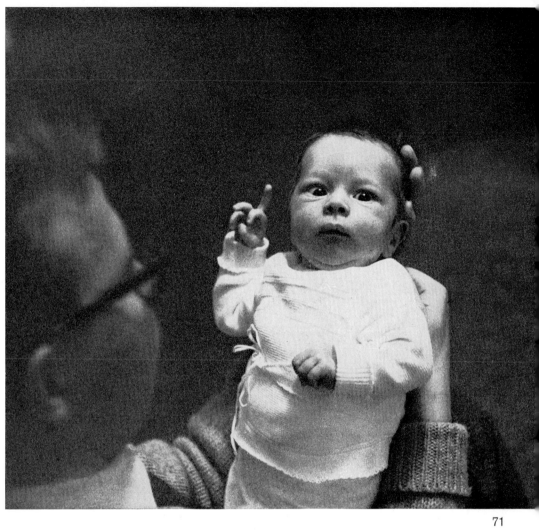

terra magica

FLIGHT

GERMANY

IRELA

FINLAND

terra magica

CHILDREN
OF
MANY
LANDS

CATS

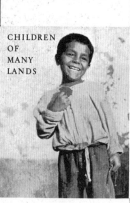

SWEDEN

DENMARK

Child
and Th
Fath

Laughing Camera

BERLIN